The EXPERT Beginner

by

Erik Dietrich

Blog Into Book
www.BlogIntoBook.com

Table of Contents

CHAPTER 1

How Developers Stop Learning: Rise of the Expert Beginner

Beyond the Dead Sea: When Good Software Groups Go Bad

In a blog post detailing what he calls the "Dead Sea Effect," Bruce Webster describes a trend whereby the most talented developers tend to be the most marketable and thus the ones most likely to leave for greener pastures when things go sour. On the other hand, the least talented developers are more likely to stay put since they'll have a hard time convincing other companies to hire them. This serves as important perspective for understanding why it's common to find people with titles like "super-duper-senior-principal-fellow-architect-awesome-dude," who make a lot of money and perhaps even wield a lot of authority but aren't very good at what they do. That perspective focuses on the individual, and many of the pages here will indeed characterize and trace the path of individual I call "the Expert Beginner." But it's also my intention to focus on software groups. The Dead Sea Effect explains the group only if one assumes that a bad group is the result of a number of these individuals happening to work in the same place—or possibly that conditions are so bad that they drive everyone except these people away.

I believe that there is a unique group dynamic that forms and causes the rot of software groups in a way that can't be explained by bad external decisions causing the talented developers to evaporate. Make no mistake—I believe that Bruce's Dead Sea Effect is both the catalyst for and the logical outcome of this dynamic. But I also believe that some magic has to happen within the group to transmute external stupidities into internal and pervasive software group incompetence. In the next chapter, I'm going to describe the mechanism by which some software groups trend toward dysfunction and professional toxicity. In this chapter, I'm going to set the stage by describing how individuals opt into permanent mediocrity and reap rewards for doing so.

Learning to Bowl

Before I get to any of that, I'd like to treat you to the history of my bowling game. Yes, I'm serious.

I am a fairly athletic person. Growing up, I was always picked at least in the top third or so of any people, for any sport or game that was being played, no matter what it was. I was a jack of all trades and master of none. This inspired in me a mildly inappropriate feeling of entitlement to skill without a lot of effort, and so it went when I became a bowler. Most people who bowl put a thumb and two fingers in the ball and carefully cultivate a method that causes the ball to start wide and hook into the middle. Having no patience for learning that, I discovered I could do a pretty good job faking it by putting no fingers and thumbs in the ball and kind of twisting my elbow and chucking the ball down the lane. It wasn't pretty, but it worked.

And actually, it worked fairly well. When I started to play in an after-work league for fun, my average started to shoot up. I wasn't the best in the league by any stretch—there were several bowlers, including a former manager of mine, who averaged between 170 and 200, but I rocketed up past 130, 140, and all the way into the 160 range within a few months of playing in the league. Not too shabby.

But then a strange thing happened. I stopped improving. Right at about 160, I topped out. I asked my old manager what I could do to get back on track with improvement, and he said something very interesting to me. Paraphrased, it was something like this:

> *There's nothing you can do to improve as long as you keep bowling like that. You've maxed out. If you want to get better, you're going to have to learn to bowl properly. You need a different ball, a different style of throwing it, and you need to put your fingers in it like a big boy. And the worst part is that you're going to get way worse before you get better, and it will be a good bit of time before you get back to and surpass your current average.*

I resisted this for a while but got bored with my lack of improvement and stagnation (a personal trait of mine—I absolutely need to be working toward mastery or I go insane) and resigned myself to the harder course. I bought a bowling ball, had it custom drilled, and started bowling properly. Ironically, I left that job almost immediately after doing that and have bowled probably eight times in the years since, but *c'est la vie*, I suppose. When I do go, I never have to rent bowling shoes or sift through the alley balls for ones that fit my fingers.

Dreyfus, Rapid Returns, and Arrested Development

In 1980, brothers Hubert and Stuart Dreyfus proposed a model of skill acquisition that has gone on to have a fair bit of influence on discussions about learning, process, and practice. Later they would go on to publish a book based on this paper and, in that book, they would refine the model a bit to its current form, as shown on Wikipedia. The model lists five phases of skill acquisition: Novice, Advanced Beginner, Competent, Proficient and Expert. There's obviously a lot to it, since it takes an entire book to describe it, but the gist of it is that skill acquirers move from "dogmatic following of rules and lack of big picture" to "intuitive transcending of rules and complete understanding of big picture."

All things being equal, one might assume that there is some sort of natural, linear advancement through these phases, like earning belts in karate, or money in the corporate world. But in reality, it doesn't shake out that way, due to both perception and attitude. At the moment one starts acquiring a skill, there is complete incompetence. This triggers an initial period of frustration and being stymied while waiting for someone, like an instructor, to spoon-feed process steps to the acquirer (or else, as Dreyfus and Dreyfus put it, they "like a baby, pick it up by imitation and floundering"). After a relatively short phase of being a complete initiate, however, one reaches a point where the skill acquisition becomes possible as a solo activity via practice, and the renewed and invigorated acquirer begins to improve quite rapidly as he or she picks "low hanging fruit." Once all that fruit is picked, however, the unsustainably rapid pace of improvement levels off somewhat, and further proficiency becomes relatively difficult from there forward. I've created a graph depicting this (which actually took me an embarrassingly long time because I messed around with plotting a variant of the logistic 1/ $(1 + e^{-x})$ function instead of drawing a line in Paint like a normal human being).

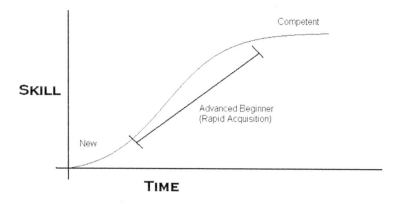

This is the exact path that my bowling game followed in my path from bowling incompetence to some degree of bowling competence. I rapidly improved to the point of competence and then completely leveled off. In my case, improvement hit a local maximum and then stopped altogether, as I was too busy to continue on my path as-is or to follow through with my retooling. This is an example of what, for the purposes of this chapter, I will call "arrested development." (I understand the overlap with a loaded psychology term, but forget that definition for a moment, please.) In the sense of skills acquisition, one generally realizes arrested development and remains at a static skill level due to one of two reasons: (1) maxing out on aptitude; or (2) some kind willingness to cease meaningful improvement.

For the remainder of this book, let's discard the first possibility, since most professional programmers wouldn't max out at or before bare minimum competence. Let's instead consider an interesting, specific instance of the second: voluntarily ceasing to improve *because of a belief that expert status has been reached and thus further improvement is not possible.* This opting into indefinite mediocrity is the entry into an oblique phase in skills acquisition that I will call the "Expert Beginner" phase.

The Expert Beginner

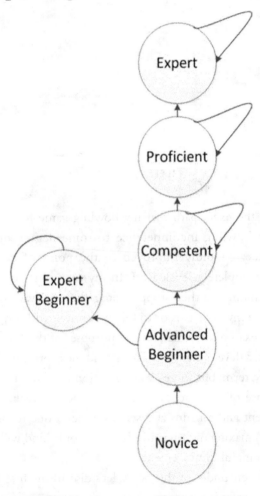

When you consider the Dreyfus model, you'll notice that there is a trend over time from being heavily rules-oriented and having no understanding of the big picture to being extremely intuitive and fully grasping the big picture. The Advanced Beginner stage is the last one in which the skill acquirer has no understanding of the big picture. As such, it's the last phase in which the acquirer might confuse himself with an Expert. A Competent has too much of a handle on the big picture to confuse himself with an Expert: he knows what he doesn't know. This isn't true during the Advanced Beginner phase, since Advanced Beginners are on the "unskilled" end of the Dunning Kruger Effect and tend to epitomize the notion, "If I don't understand it, it must be easy."

As such, Advanced Beginners can break one of two ways: they can move to Competent and start to grasp the big picture and their place in it, or they can 'graduate' to Expert Beginner by assuming that they've graduated to Expert. This isn't as immediately ridiculous as it sounds.

Let's go back to my erstwhile bowling career and consider what might have happened had I been the only or best bowler in the alley. I would have started out doing poorly and then quickly picked the low hanging fruit of skill acquisition to rapidly advance. Dunning-Kruger notwithstanding, I might have rationally concluded that I had a pretty good aptitude for bowling as my skill level grew quickly. And I might also have concluded somewhat rationally (if rather arrogantly) that me leveling off indicated that I had reached the pinnacle of bowling skill. After all, I don't see anyone around me that's better than me, and there must be some point of mastery, so I guess I'm there.

The real shame of this is that a couple of inferences that aren't entirely irrational lead me to a false feeling of achievement and then spur me on to opt out of further improvement. I go from my optimistic self-assessment to a logical fallacy as my bowling career continues: "I know that I'm doing it right because, as an Expert, I'm pretty much doing everything right by definition." (For you logical fallacy buffs, this is circular reasoning/begging the question).

Looking at the graphic above, you'll notice that it depicts a state machine of the Dreyfus model as you would expect it. At each stage, one might either progress to the next one or remain in the current one (with the exception of Novice or Advanced Beginner, who I feel can't really remain at that phase without abandoning the activity). The difference is that I've added the Expert Beginner to the chart as well.

The Expert Beginner has nowhere to go because progression requires an understanding that he has a lot of work to do, and that is not a readily available conclusion. You'll notice that the Expert Beginner is positioned slightly above Advanced Beginner but not on the level of Competence. This is because he is not competent enough to grasp the big picture and recognize the irony of his situation, but he is slightly more competent than the Advanced Beginner due mainly to, well, extensive practice being a Beginner. If you've ever heard the aphorism about "ten years of experience or the same year of experience ten times," the Expert Beginner is the epitome of the latter. The Expert Beginner has perfected the craft of bowling a 160 out of 300 possible points by doing exactly the same thing week in and week out with no significant deviations from routine or desire to experiment. This is because he believes that 160 is the best possible score by virtue of the fact that he scored it.

Expert Beginners in Software

Software is, unsurprisingly, not like bowling. In bowling, feedback cycles are on the order of minutes, whereas in software, feedback cycles tend to be on the order of months, if not years. And what I'm talking about with software is not the feedback cycle of compile or run or unit tests, which *is* minutes or seconds, but rather of the project. It's during the full lifetime of a project that a developer gains experience writing code, source controlling it, modifying it, testing it and living with previous design and architecture decisions during maintenance phases. With everything I've just described, a developer is lucky to have a first try of less than six months, which means that, after five years in the industry, maybe they have ten cracks at application development. (This is on average—some will be stuck on a single one the whole time while others will have dozens.)

What this means is that the rapid acquisition phase of a software developer—Advanced Beginnerism—will last for years rather than weeks. And during these years, software developers are job-hopping and earning promotions, especially these days. As they breeze through rapid acquisition, so too do they breeze through titles like Software Engineer I and II and then maybe "Associate" and "Senior," and perhaps eventually on up to "Lead" and "Architect" and "Principal." So while in the throes of Dunning-Kruger and Advanced Beginnerism, they're being given Expert-sounding titles and told that they're rock stars and ninjas by recruiters, especially in today's economy. The only thing stopping them from taking the natural step into the Expert Beginner stage is a combination of peer review and interaction with the development community at large.

But what happens when the Advanced Beginner doesn't care enough to interact with the broader community and for whatever reason doesn't have much interaction with peers? The Daily WTF is filled with such examples. They fail even while convinced that the failure is everyone else's fault, and the nature of the game is such that blaming others is easy and handy to relieve any cognitive dissonance. They come to the conclusion that they've quickly reached Expert status and there's nowhere left to go. They've officially become Expert Beginners, and they're ready to entrench themselves into some niche in an organization and collect a huge paycheck because no one around them, including them, realizes that they can do a lot better.

And so we have chronicled the rise of the Expert Beginner: where they come from and why they stop progressing. In the next chapter, I will explore the mechanics by which one or more Expert Beginners create a degenerative situation in which they actively cause festering and rot in the dynamics of groups that have talented members or could otherwise be healthy.

CHAPTER 2

How Software Groups Rot: Legacy of the Expert Beginner

Expansion on a Definition

The term "Expert Beginner" describes someone who has capped out in their learning at a local maximum, convinced that the local is global. Expert Beginners are developers who do not understand enough of the big picture to understand that they aren't actually experts. What I mean by this is that they have a narrow enough perspective to think that whatever they have been exposed to is the best and only way to do things. Examples include a C# developer who pooh-poohs Java without ever having tried it or a MySQL DBA who dismisses the NoSQL movement as a passing fad. This isn't to say that not liking a technology or not having worked with one makes someone an Expert Beginner. Rather, it's the vaguely solipsistic mindset of "if it's not in my toolchest or something I've had experience with, it's not worth doing" that puts a person in this category.

Another characteristic of Expert Beginners, however, is that they have some position of relative authority or influence within a software group. In my last chapter, I proposed the term Expert

Beginner without giving the rationale for the name. I'll explain that now. While the *Advanced* Beginner is someone who is in the advanced stage of being a beginner, the *Expert* Beginner descriptor is both literal and intentionally ironic; it's literal in that someone with that much practice at being a beginner could only be said to be an expert, and it's ironic in that the "expert" title is generally self-applied in earnest or else applied by managers or peers who don't know any better.

The iconic example might be the "tech guy" at a small, non-technical firm. He "knows computers," so as the company grew and evolved to have some mild IT needs, he became a programming dilettante out of necessity. In going from being a power user to being a developer, his skills exceeded his expectations, so he became confident in his limited, untrained abilities. Absent any other peers in the field, the only people there to evaluate his skills are himself and non-technical users who offer such lofty praises as "it seems to work, kind of, I think." He is the one-eyed man in the valley of the blind and, in a very real and unfortunate sense, a local expert. This is the iconic example because it has the fewest barriers to Expert Beginnerism—success is simple, standards are low, actual experts are absent, competition is non-existent, and external interaction is not a given.

A Single Point of Rot...

So far I've talked a lot about the Expert Beginner—his emergence, his makeup, his mindset, and a relatively sympathetic explanation of the pseudo-rationality, or at least understandability, of his outlook. But how does this translate into support of my original thesis that Expert Beginners cause professional toxicity and degeneration of software groups? To explain that, I'm going to return to my bowling analogy from chapter 1, and please bear with me if the metaphor is a touch strained.

Let's say that bowling alleys make their money by how well their bowlers bowl and that I live in a small town with a little startup bowling alley. Not being able to find any work as a software developer, I try my hand bowling at the local alley. I don't really know what I'm doing and neither do they, but we both see me improving rapidly as I start bowling there, in spite of my goofy style. My average goes up, the bowling alley makes money, and life is good—there's no arguing with profit and success!

Around about the time my score was topping 150 and the sky seemed the limit, the bowling alley decided that it was time to expand and to hire a couple of entry-level bowlers to work under my tutelage. On the day they arrived, I showed them how to hold the ball just like I hold it and how to walk just like I do. When they ask what the thumb and finger holes are for, I respond by saying, "Don't worry about those—we don't use them here." Eager to please, they listen to me and see their averages increase the way mine had, even as I'm starting to top out at around a 160 average.

As time goes by, most of them are content to do things my way. But a couple are ambitious and start to practice during their spare time. They read books and watch shows on bowling technique. One day, these ambitious bowlers come in and say, "The guys on TV put their fingers in the ball, and they get some really high averages–over

200!" They expect me to be as interested as they are in the prospect of improvement and are crestfallen when I respond with, "No, that's just not how we do things here. I've been bowling for longer than you've been alive and I know what I'm doing... besides, you can't believe everything you see on TV."

And thus, quickly and decisively, I squash innovation for the group by reminding them that I'm in charge by virtue of having been at the bowling alley for longer than they have. This is a broadly accepted yet totally inadequate non sequitur that stops discussion without satisfying. At this point, half of the ambitious developers abandon their "fingers in the ball" approach while the other half meet after work at another alley and practice it together in semi-secret. After a while, their averages reach and surpass mine, and they assume that this development—this objective demonstration of the superiority of their approach—will result in a change in the way things are done. When it instead results in anger and lectures and claims that the scores were a fluke and I, too, once bowled a 205 that one time, they evaporate and leave the residue behind. They leave my dead-end, backward bowling alley for a place where people don't favor demonstrably inferior approaches out of stubbornness.

The bowling alley loses its highest-average bowlers not to another alley, but to an Expert Beginner.

...That Poisons the Whole

The bowlers who don't leave learn two interesting lessons from this. The first lesson they learn is that if they wait their turn, they can wield unquestioned authority regardless of merit. The second lesson they learn is that it's okay and even preferred to be mediocre at this alley. So when new bowlers are hired, in the interests of toeing the company line and waiting their turn, they participate in the inculcation of bad practices to the newbies the same way as was done to them. The Expect Beginner has, through his actions and example, created additional Expert Beginners and has, in fact, created a culture of Expert Beginnerism.

The other interesting development comes in the acquisition process. As the Expert-Beginner-in-Chief, I've learned a pointed lesson. Since I don't like being shown up by ambitious young upstarts, I begin to alter my recruitment process to look for mediocre "team players" that won't threaten my position with their pie-in-the-sky "fingers in the ball" ideas. Now, I know what you're thinking—doesn't this level of awareness belie the premise of the Expert Beginner being unaware of the big picture? The answer is no. This hiring decision is more subconscious and rationalized than overt. It isn't, "I won't hire people that are better than me," but, "those people just aren't a good fit here with my 'outside the box' and 'expert' way of doing things." And it may even be that I'm so ensconced in Expert Beginnerism that I confuse Competent/Expert level work with incompetent work because I don't know any better. (The bowling analogy breaks down a bit here, but it might be on par with a "bowling interview" in which I just watched the form of the interviewee's throw, not the results, and then concluded that the form of a 220 bowler was bad because it was different than my own.) And, in doing all this, I'm reinforcing the culture for everyone including my new Expert Beginner lieutenants.

Now the bowling alley is losing all of its potentially high-average bowlers to a cabal of Expert Beginners. Also notice that Bruce Webster's Dead Sea Effect is fully mature and realized at this point.

Back in the Real World

That's all well and good for bowling and bowling alleys, but how is this comparable to real software development practices? Well, it's relatively simple. Perhaps it's a lack of automated testing. Giant methods/classes. Lots of copy-and-paste coding. Use of outdated or poor tooling. Process. It can be any number of things, but the common thread is that you have a person or people in positions of authority that have the culturally lethal combination of not knowing much; not knowing what they don't know; and assuming that, due to their own expertise, anything they don't know isn't worth knowing. This is a toxic professional culture in that it will force talented or ambitious people either to leave or to conform to mediocrity.

You may think that this is largely a function of individual personalities—that departments become this way by having arrogant or pushy incompetents in charge. I think it's more subtle than that. These Expert Beginners may not have such personality defects at all. I think it's a natural conclusion of insular environments, low expectations, and ongoing rewards for mediocre and/or unquantifiable performances. And think about the nature of our industry. How many outfits have you worked at where there is some sort of release party, even (or especially) when the release is over budget, buggy, and behind schedule? How many outfits have you worked at that gave up on maintaining some unruly beast of an application in favor of a complete rewrite, only to repeat that cycle later? And the people involved in this receive accolades and promotions, which would be like promoting rocket makers for making rockets that looked functional but simply stopped and fell back to earth after a few hundred feet. "Well, that didn't work, Jones, but you learned a lot from it, so we're promoting you to Principal Rocket Builder and having you lead version two, you rock star, you!" Is it any wonder that Jones starts to think of himself as King Midas?

As an industry, we get away with this because people have a substantially lower expectation of software than they do of rockets. I'm not saying this to complain or to suggest sweeping change but rather to explain how it's easy for us to think that we're further along in our skills acquisition than we actually are, based on both our own perception and external feedback.

CHAPTER 3

≈

How Stagnation is Justified: Language of the Expert Beginner

Words Speak Louder than Actions

So far, I've chronicled how Expert Beginners emerge and how they wind up infecting an entire software development group. In this chapter, I'd like to turn my attention to the rhetoric of this archetype in a software group already suffering from Expert-Beginner-induced rot. In other words, I'm going to discuss how Expert Beginners who are deeply entrenched in their lairs interact with newbies to the department.

It's no accident that this chapter specifically mentions the language rather than interpersonal interactions of the Expert Beginner. The reason is that the actions aren't particularly remarkable. They resemble the actions of any tenured employee, line manager, or person in a position of company trust. These folks delegate, call the shots, set policy, and probably engage in status posturing, playing chicken with meeting lateness or sitting with their feet on the table when talking to those of lesser organizational status. Experts and Expert Beginners are pretty hard to tell apart based exclusively on how they behave. It's the language that provides a fascinating tell.

Most people, when arguing a position, will cite some combination of facts and deductive or inductive reasoning, perhaps with the occasional logical fallacy sprinkled in by mistake. For instance, "I left the windows open because I wanted to air out the house and I didn't realize it was supposed to rain," describes a choice and the rationale for it with an implied *mea culpa*. The Expert Beginner takes a fundamentally different approach, and that's what I'll be exploring here.

False Tradeoffs and Empty Valuations

If you're cynical or intelligent with a touch of arrogance, there's an expression you're likely to find funny. It's a little too ubiquitous for me to be sure who originally coined the phrase, but if anyone knows, I'm happy to amend and offer an original source attribution. The phrase is this: "Whenever someone says 'I'm not book smart, but I'm street smart,' all I hear is, 'I'm not real smart, but I'm imaginary smart.'" I had a bit of a chuckle the first time I read that, but it's not actually what I, personally, think when I hear people describe themselves as "street smart" rather than "book smart." What I think is being communicated is "I'm not book smart, and I'm sort of sensitive about that, so I'd like that particular valuation of people not to be emphasized by society." Or, more succinctly, "I'm not book smart, and I want that not to be held against me."

"Street smart" is, at its core, a counterfeit status currency proffered in lieu of a legitimate one. It has meaning only in the context of it being accepted as a stand-in for the real McCoy. If I get the sense that you're considering accepting me into your club based on the quantity of "smarts" that I have and I'm not particularly confident that I can come up with the ante, I offer you some worthless thing called "street smarts" and claim that it's of equal replacement value. If you decide to accept this currency, then I win. And, interestingly, if enough other people decide to accept it, then it becomes a real form of currency (which I think it'd be pretty easy to argue that "street smart" has).

Whatever you may think of the book smart versus street smart dichotomy notwithstanding, you'd be hard pressed to argue that the transaction doesn't follow the pattern of "I want X," "I don't have that, but I have Y (and I'm claiming Y is just as good)." And understanding this attempted substitution is key to understanding one of the core planks of the language of Expert Beginners. They are extremely adept at creating empty valuations as stand-ins for meaningful ones. To see this in action, consider the following:

1. Version control isn't really that important if you have a good architecture and two people never have to touch the same file.
2. We don't write unit tests because our developers spend extra time inspecting the code after they've written it.
3. Yeah, we don't do a lot of Java here, but you can do anything with Perl that you can with Java.
4. Our build may not be automated, but it's very scientific, and there's a lot of complicated stuff that requires an expert to do manually.
5. We don't need to be agile or iterative because we write requirements really well.
6. We save a lot of money by not splurging on productivity add-ins and fancy development environments, and it makes our programmers more independent.

In all cases here, the pattern is the same. The Expert Beginner takes something that's considered an industry standard or best practice, admits to not practicing it, and offers instead something completely unacceptable (or even nonsensical/made up) as a stand-in, implying that you should accept the switch because they say so.

Condescension and Devaluations

This language tactic is worth only a brief mention because it's pretty obvious as a ploy, and it squanders a lot of realpolitik capital in the office if anyone is paying attention. It's basically the domain-specific equivalent of some idiot being interviewed on the local news, just before dying of hurricane, saying something like, "I'm not gonna let a buncha fancy Harvard science guys tell me about storms—I've lived here for forty years and I can feel 'emcomin' in my bones. If I need to evacuate, I'll know it!"

In his fiefdom, an Expert Beginner is obligated to have some explanation for ignoring best practices that at least rises to the level of sophistry and offers some sort of explanation, however improbable. This is where last section's false valuations shine. Simply scoffing at best practices and new ideas has to be done sparingly, or upper management will start to notice and create uncomfortable situations. And besides, this reaction is frankly beneath the average Expert Beginner—it's how a frustrated and petulant Novice would react. Still, it will occasionally be trotted out in a pinch and can be effective in that usage scenario since it requires no brain cells and will just be interpreted as passion rather than intellectual laziness.

The Angry Driver Effect

If you ever watch a truly surly driver on the highway, you'll notice an interesting bit of irritable cognitive bias against literally everyone else on the road. The driver will shake her fist at motorists passing her, calling them "maniacs," while shaking the same fist at those going more slowly, calling them "putzes." There's simply no pleasing her.

An Expert Beginner employs this tactic with all members of the group as well, although without the anger. For example, if she has a master's degree, she will characterize solutions put forth by those with bachelor's degrees as lacking formal polish, while simultaneously characterizing those put forth by people with PhDs as overly academic or out of touch. If the solution different from hers is presented by someone that also has a master's, she will pivot to another subject.

Is your solution one that she understands immediately? Too simplistic. Does she not understand it? Over-engineered and convoluted. Are you younger than her? It's full of rookie mistakes. Older? Out of touch and hackneyed. Did you take longer than it would have taken her? You're inefficient. Did it take you less time? You're careless. She will keep pivoting, as needed, *ad infinitum*.

Taken individually, any one of these characterizations makes sense and impresses. In a way, it's like the cold-reading game that psychics play. Here the trick is to identify a personal difference and characterize anything produced by its owner as negative. The Expert Beginner controls the location of the goalposts via framing in the same way that the psychic rattles off a series of 'predictions' until one is right, as evidenced by micro-expressions. The actual subtext is, "I'm in charge and I get to define good and bad, so good is me, and some amount less good is you."

Interestingly, the Expert Beginner's definition of good versus bad is completely orthogonal to any external characterizations of the same. For instance, if the Expert Beginner had been a C student, in her group, D students would be superior to A students because of their relative proximity to the ideal C student. The D students might be "humble, but a little slow," while A students would be "blinded by their own arrogance," or some such thing. It's completely irrelevant that society at large considers A students to be of the most value.

Experts are Wrong

Given that Expert Beginners are of mediocre ability by definition, the subject of expertise is a touchy one. Within the small group, this isn't really a problem since the Expert Beginner is the designated expert there. But within a larger scope, actual Experts at the top of the Dreyfus model exist, and they present a problem—particularly when group members are exposed to them and realize that discrepancies exist.

For instance, let's say that an Expert Beginner in a small group has never bothered with source control for code due to laziness and a simple lack of exposure. This decision is likely settled case law within the group, having been justified with something like the "good architecture" canard from the Empty Valuations section. But if any group member watches a Pluralsight video or attends a conference which exposes them to industry experts and best practices, the conflict becomes immediately apparent and will be brought to the attention of the reigning Expert Beginner. In the last chapter, I made a brief example of an Expert Beginner reaction to such a situation: "You can't believe everything you see on TV."

This is the simplest and most straightforward reaction to such a situation. The Expert Beginner believes that he and his 'fellow' Expert have a simple difference of opinion among 'peers.' While it may be true that one Expert speaks at conferences about source control best practices and the other one runs the IT for Bill's Bait Shop and has never used source control, either opinion is just as valid. But on a long enough timeline, this false relativism falls apart due to mounting disagreement between the Expert Beginner and real Experts.

When this happens, the natural bit of nuance that Expert Beginners introduce is exceptionalism. Rather than saying, "well, source control or not, either one is fine," and risk looking like the oddball, the Expert Beginner invents a mitigating circumstance that would not apply to other Experts, effectively creating an argument that he can win by forfeit. (None of his opponents are aware of his existence and thus offer no counterargument.) For instance, Bill's Bait Shop's Expert Beginner might say, "sure, those Experts are right that source control is a good idea in most cases, but they don't understand the bait industry."

This is a pretty effective master stroke. The actual Experts have been dressed down for their lack of knowledge of the bait industry while the Expert Beginner is sitting pretty as the most informed one of the bunch. And, best of all, none of the actual Experts are aware of this argument, so none of them will bother to poke holes in it. Crisis averted.

All Qualitative Comparisons Lead Back to Seniority

A final arrow in the Expert Beginner debate quiver is the simple tactic of non sequitur about seniority, tenure, or company experience. On the surface this would seem like the most contrived and least credible ploy possible, but it's surprisingly effective in corporate culture, where seniority is the default currency in the economy of developmental promotions. Most denizens of the corporate world automatically assign value and respect to "years with the company."

Since there is no bigger beneficiary of this phenomenon than an Expert Beginner, he plows investment into it in an attempt to drive the market price as high as possible. If you ask the Expert Beginner why there is no automated build process, he might respond with something like, "you'll understand after you've worked here for a while." If you ask him this potentially embarrassing question in front of others, he'll up the ante to "I asked that once too when I was new and naive—you have a lot to learn," at which time anyone present is required by corporate etiquette to laugh at the newbie and nervously reaffirm that value is directly proportional to months employed by Acme Inc.

The form and delivery of this particular tactic will vary a good bit, but the pattern is the same at a meta-level. State your conclusion, invent a segue, and subtly remind everyone present that you've been there the longest. "We tried the whole TDD thing way back in 2005, and I think all of the senior developers and project managers know how poorly that went." "Migrating from VB6 to something more modern definitely sounds like a good idea at first, but there are some VPs you haven't met that aren't going to buy that one."

It goes beyond simple non sequitur. This tactic serves as a thinly veiled reminder as to who calls the shots. It's a message that says, "here's a gentle reminder that I've been here a long time and I don't need to justify things to the likes of you." Most people receive this Expert Beginner message loudly and clearly and start to join in, hopeful for the time they can point the business end at someone else as part of the "Greater Newbie Theory."

Ab Hominem

In the beginning of this chapter, I talked about the standard means for making and/or defending arguments (deductive or inductive reasoning) and how Expert Beginners do something else altogether. I've provided a lot of examples of it, but I haven't actually defined it. The central feature of the Expert Beginner's influence-consolidation language is an inextricable fusing of arguer and argument, which is the polar opposite of standard argument form. For instance, it doesn't matter who says, "if all humans have hearts, and Jim is a human, then Jim has a heart." The argument stands on its own. But it *does* matter who says, "those of us who've been around for a while would know why not bothering to define requirements is actually better than SCRUM." That argument is preposterous from an outsider or a newbie but acceptable from an Expert Beginner.

A well-formed argument says, "if you think about this, you'll find it persuasive." The language of the Expert Beginner says, "it's better if you don't think about this—just remember who I am, and that's all you need to know." This can be overt, such as with the seniority dropping, or it can be more subtle, such as with empty valuations. It can also be stacked so that a gentle non sequitur can be followed with a nastier "get off of my lawn" type of dressing down if the first message is not received.

In the end, it all makes perfect sense. Expert Beginners arrive at their stations by default rather than merit. As such, they have basically no practice at persuading anyone to see the value of their ideas or at demonstrating the superiority of their approach. Instead, the only thing they can offer is the evidence that they have of their qualifications—their relative position of authority. And so, during any arguments or explanations, all roads lead back to them, their position titles, their time with the company, and the fact that their opinions are inviolate.

CHAPTER 4

Up or Not: Ambition of the Expert Beginner

Cognitive Dissonance, Revisited

In general, I've talked about how Expert Beginners get started, become established, and, most recently, about how they fend off new ideas (read: threats) in order to retain their status with minimal effort. But what I haven't yet covered and will now talk about is the motivations and goals of the Expert Beginner. Obviously, motivation is a complex subject, and motivations will be as varied as individuals. But I believe that Expert Beginner ambition can be roughly categorized into groups and that these groups are a function of their tolerance for cognitive dissonance.

Wikipedia (and other places) defines cognitive dissonance as mental discomfort that arises from simultaneously holding conflicting beliefs. For instance, someone who really likes the taste of steak but believes that it's unethical to eat meat will experience this form of unsettling stress as he tries to reconcile these ultimately irreconcilable beliefs. Different people have different levels of discomfort that arise from this state of affairs, and this applies to Expert Beginners as much as anyone else. What makes Expert Beginners unique, however, is how inescapable cognitive dissonance is for them.

An Expert Beginner's entire career is built on a foundation of cognitive dissonance. Specifically, they believe they are experts while outside observers (or empirical evidence) demonstrate they are not. So an Expert Beginner is sentenced to a life of believing himself to be an expert while all evidence points to the contrary, punctuated by frequent and extremely unwelcome intrusions of that reality.

So let's consider three classes of Expert Beginner, distinguished by their tolerance for cognitive dissonance and their paths through an organization.

Xenophobes (Low Tolerance)

An Expert Beginner with a low tolerance for cognitive dissonance is basically in a state of existential crisis, given that he has a low tolerance for the thing that characterizes his career. To put this more concretely, a marginally competent person inaccurately dubbed "Expert" by his organization is going to be generally unhappy if he has little ability to reconcile or accept conflicting beliefs. A more robust Expert Beginner has the ability to dismiss evidence against his "Expert" status as wrong, but not Xenophobe. Xenophobe becomes angry, distressed, or otherwise moody when this sort of thing happens.

But Xenophobe's long term strategy isn't simply to get worked up whenever something exposes his knowledge gap. Instead, he minimizes his exposure to such situations. This process of minimizing is where the name Xenophobe originates; he shelters himself from cognitive dissonance by sheltering himself from outsiders and interlopers that expose him to it.

If you've been to enough rodeos in the field of software development, you've encountered Xenophobe. He generally presides over a small group with an iron fist. He'll have endless reams of coding standards, procedures, policies, rules, and quirky ways of doing things that are non-negotiable and soul-sucking. This is accompanied by an intense dose of micromanagement and insistence on absolute conformity in all matters. Nothing escapes his watchful eye, and his management generally views this as dedication or even, perversely, mentoring.

This practice of micromanagement serves double duty for Xenophobe. Most immediately, it allows him largely to prevent the group from being infected by any foreign ideas. On the occasion that one does sneak in, his vigilance allows him to eliminate it swiftly and ruthlessly, and he will take steps to prevent the same perpetrator from doing it again. But on a longer timeline, the oppressive micromanagement systematically drives out talented subordinates in favor of malleable, disinterested ones that are fine with brainlessly banging out code from nine to five, asking no questions, and listening to the radio. Xenophobe's group is the epitome of what Bruce Webster describes in his Dead Sea Effect post.

All that Xenophobe wants out of life is to preserve this state of affairs. Any meaningful change to the status quo is a threat to his iron-fisted rule over his little kingdom. He doesn't want anyone to leave because that probably means new hires, which are potential sources of contamination. He will similarly resist external pushes to change the group and its mission. New business ventures will be labeled "unfeasible" or "not what we do."

Most people working in corporate structures want to move up at some point. This is generally because doing so means higher pay, but it's also because it comes with additional status perks like offices, parking spaces, and the mandate to boss people around. Xenophobe is not interested in any of this, beyond whatever he already has. He simply wants to come in every day and be regarded as the alpha technical expert. Moving up to management would result in whatever goofy architecture and infrastructure he's set up being systematically dismantled, and his ego couldn't handle that. So he demurs in the face of any promotion to project management or real management because even beneficial changes would poke holes in the Expert delusion. You'll hear Xenophobe say things like, "I'd never want to take my hands off the keyboard, man," or, "this company would never survive me moving to management."

Company Men (Moderate Tolerance)

Company Man does not share Xenophobe's reluctance to move into a line or middle management role. His comfort with this move results from being somewhat more at peace with cognitive dissonance. He isn't so consumed with preserving the illusion of expertise at all costs that he'll pass up potential benefits—he's a more rational and less pathological kind of Expert Beginner.

Generally speaking, the line to a mid-level management position requires some comfort with cognitive dissonance whether or not the manager came into power from the ranks of technical Expert Beginners. Organizations are generally shaped like pyramids, with executives at the top, a larger layer of management in the middle, and line employees at the bottom. It shares more than just shape with a pyramid scheme–it sells to the rank and file the idea that ascension to the top is inevitable provided they work hard and serve those above them well.

The source of cognitive dissonance in the middle, however, isn't simply the numerical impossibility that everyone can work their way up. Rather, the dissonance lies in the belief that working your way up has much to do with merit or talent. In other words, only the daftest employee would believe that everyone will inevitably wind up in the CEO's office (or even in middle management), so the idea most buy into is this: each step of the pyramid selects its members from the most worthy of the step below it. The 'best' line employees become line managers, the 'best' line managers become mid-level managers, and so on up the pyramid. This is a pleasant fiction for members of the company that, when believed, inspires company loyalty and often hard work beyond what makes rational sense for a salaried employee.

But the reality is that mid-level positions tend to be occupied not necessarily by the talented but rather by people who have stuck around the company for a long time, people who are friends with or related to movers and shakers in the company, people who put in long hours, people who simply and randomly got lucky, and people who legitimately get work done effectively. So while there's a myth perpetuated in corporate American that ascending the corporate 'ladder' (pyramid) is a matter of achievement, it's really more of a matter of age and inevitability, at least until you get high enough into the C-level where there simply aren't enough positions for token promotions. If you don't believe me, go look at LinkedIn and tell me that there isn't an intensely strong correlation between age and impressiveness of title.

So, to occupy a middle management position is almost invariably to drastically overestimate how much talent and achievement it took to get to where you are. That may sound harsh, but "I worked hard and put in long hours and eventually worked my way up to an office next to the corner office" is a much more pleasant narrative than "I stuck with this company, shoveled crap, and got older until enough people left to make this office more or less inevitable." But what does all of this have to do with Expert Beginners?

Well, Expert Beginners that are moderately tolerant of cognitive dissonance have approximately the same level of tolerance for it as middle management, which is to say they have a fair amount. Both sets manage to believe that their positions were earned through merit while empirical evidence points to them getting there by default and managing not to fumble it away. Thus it's a relatively smooth transition, from a cognitive dissonance perspective, for a technical Expert Beginner to become a manager. They simply trade technical mediocrity for managerial mediocrity and the narrative writes itself: "I was so good at being a software architect that I've earned a shot and will be good at being a manager."

The Xenophobe would never get to that point because asking him to mimic competence at a new skill-set is going to draw him outside of his comfort zone. He views moving into management as a tacit admission that he was in over his head and needed to be promoted out of danger. Company Man has no such compunction. He's not comfortable or happy when people in his group bring in outside information or threaten to expose his relative incompetence, but he's not nearly as vicious and reactionary as Xenophobe, as he can tolerate the odd creeping doubt of his total expertise.

In fact, he'll often alleviate this doubt by crafting an "up after a while" story for himself vis-a-vis management. You'll hear him say things like, "I'm getting older and can't keep slinging code forever—sooner or later, I'll probably just have to go into management." It seems affable enough, but he's really planning a face-saving exit strategy. When you start out not quite competent and insulate yourself from actual competence in a fast-changing field like software, failure is inevitable. Company Man knows this on some subconscious level, so he plans and aspires to a victorious retreat. This continues as high as Company Man is able to rise in the organization (though non-strategic thinkers are unlikely to rise much above line manager, generally). He's comfortable with enough cognitive dissonance at every level that he doesn't let not being competent stop him from assuming that he is competent.

Master Beginners (High Tolerance)

If Xenophobes want to stay put and Company Men want to advance, you would think that the class of people who have a high tolerance for and thus no problem with cognitive dissonance, Master Beginners, would chomp at the bit to advance. But from an organizational perspective, they really don't. Their desired trajectory from an org chart perspective is somewhere between Xenophobe and Company Man. Specifically, they prefer to stay put in a technical role but to expand their sphere of influence, breadth-wise—to grow the technical group under their tutelage. Perhaps at some point they'd be satisfied to be CTO or VP of Engineering or something, but only as long as they didn't get too far away from their domain of 'expertise.'

Master Beginners are utterly fascinating. I've only ever encountered a few of these in my career, but it's truly a memorable experience. Xenophobes are very much Expert Beginners by nurture rather than nature. They're normal people who backed their way into a position for which they aren't fit and thus have to either admit defeat (and, worse, that their main accomplishment in life is being in the right place at the right time) or neurotically preserve their delusion by force. Company Men are also Expert Beginners by nurture over nature, though for them it's less localized than Xenophobes. Company Men buy into the broader lie that advancement in command-and-control bureaucratic organizations is a function of merit. If a hole is poked in that delusion, they may fall, but a lot of others come with them. It's a more stable fiction.

But Master Beginners are somehow Expert Beginners by nature. They are the meritocratic equivalent of sociopaths in that their incredible tolerance for cognitive dissonance allows them glibly and with an astonishing lack of shame to feign expertise when doing so is preposterous. It appears on the surface to be utter, stunning arrogance. A Master Beginner would stand up in front of a room full of Java programmers, never having written a line of Java code in his life, and proceed to explain to them the finer points of Java, literally making things up as he went. But it's so brazen—so completely beyond reason—that arrogance, though no doubt a component of his personality, is not a sufficient explanation. It's as if the Master Beginner is a pathological liar of some kind. He actually believes that he knows more about subjects of which he has no understanding than legitimate experts in those fields because he's just that brilliant.

This makes him an excellent candidate for Expert Beginnerism both from an external, non-technical perspective and from a rookie perspective. To put it bluntly, both rookies and outside managers listen to him and think, "wow, that must be true because nobody would have the balls to talk like that unless they were absolutely certain." This actually tends to make him better at Expert Beginnerism than his cohorts who are more sensitive to cognitive dissonance, roughly following the psychological phenomenon coined by Walter Langer:

> *People will believe a big lie sooner than a little one. And if you repeat it frequently enough, people will sooner than later believe it.*

So the Master Beginner's ambition isn't to slither his way out of situations that might cause him to be called out for his lack. He actually embraces them. The Master Beginner is utterly unflappable in his status as not just an Expert, but *the* Expert, completely confident that things he just invents are more right than things others have studied for years. Thus the Master Beginner seeks to expand aggressively. He wants to grow the department and bring more people under his authority. He'll back down from no challenge to his authority from any angle, glibly inventing things on the spot to win any argument, pivoting, spinning, shouting, threatening—whatever the situation calls for. And he won't stop until everyone hails him as the resident Expert and does everything his way.

Success?

I've talked about the ambitions of different kinds of Expert Beginners and what drives them to aspire to these ends. But a worthwhile question to ask is whether or not they tend to succeed and why or why not. I'm going to tackle the fate of Expert Beginners in greater detail in the next chapter, but the answer is, of course, that it varies. What tends not to vary, however, is that Expert Beginner success is generally high in the short term and drops to nearly zero on a long enough time line, at least in terms of their ambitions. In other words, success as measured by Expert Beginners themselves tends to be somewhat ephemeral.

It stands to reason that being deluded about one's own competence isn't a viable, long-term success strategy. There is a lesson to be learned from the fate of Expert Beginners in general, which is that better outcomes would be more likely if they had an honest valuation of their own talents and skills. As it stands, Expert Beginners live on borrowed time.

CHAPTER 5

≈≈≈

Self-Correcting Organizations:
Fall of the Expert Beginner

The Human Cost

If you've purchased this book, it's pretty likely that you too have observed/ or dealt with Expert Beginners. That is, you've most likely encountered someone like this in your travels and been stymied, belittled, annoyed, exasperated, etc. by this Expert Beginner. So you're probably rooting for the outcome in the title of the chapter. This is the point at which the cosmic scales are rebalanced and the arrogant Expert Beginner finally gets his comeuppance: the fall of the Expert Beginner. But not so fast—there's some ground to cover first, and if you're looking for a nice resolution where the bad guy is brought to justice, you might be disappointed.

I mean, it's nice to read the Daily WTF and see the occasional story about a bungling-but-nasty manager or architect being dressed down or laid off. But in your life the players involved are actual people, and everyone suffers real consequences. If you hire on with an organization dominated by an Expert Beginner and then leave in frustration, you're investing time that you'll never get back and incurring the hassle of a job search sooner than expected. You also probably came on board because you liked the company and its goals and mission. Now you leave knowing that its interests are being sabotaged by incompetence and that your friends and everyone else still working there are not doing as well as they could be if the company were enjoying more success. And even if the Expert Beginner does wind up being disgraced somehow, via demotion or termination, that's a person who now must explain to a family that they're going to have to batten down the hatches financially until he figures something out.

Escaping Intact

In the last chapter, I said that Expert Beginners generally enjoy high odds for short term success which drop to zero on a long enough timeline. Here, I'd like to talk about the means by which some Expert Beginners tend to escape that fate before describing it in detail.

The secret to success in the Expert Beginner world is to understand that programming (or really any line-level expertise) has to be a means to an end only. It's not a skill that you're going to master, but one of which you'll fake mastery for just long enough to profit (literally and figuratively) and bail out. This requires some ability to both tolerate cognitive dissonance and swallow pride, albeit in a way that allows for ample spinning of the truth. And, really, there's only one category of Expert Beginner from the three that I defined in the previous chapter that can get out of the game as a success: the Company Man.

Let's consider casino poker as a metaphor for explaining the fate of Expert Beginners. Expert Beginners are essentially poker novices who sit down at a low stakes table, catch a run of incredible cards, and wind up with a big fat stack through the vagaries of chance. From there, the paths diverge depending on the archetype.

Xenophobe stays at the low stakes table because on some level he knows that he'll get slaughtered by good players at the high stakes tables. He doesn't tell himself this, naturally, but rather insists that he likes the down-to-earth vibe of the table or something. He also doesn't cash out because being good at poker is important to him. So he rides his initial luck as far as it will go, but, sooner or later, that luck runs out. Slowly he loses control of his modest fortune, one bad bet and wrong play at a time, until he's chip-less. He eventually leaves with nothing in his pocket, unable to understand why repeating the exact behaviors that earned him success didn't continue to work.

Master Beginner takes his initial luck and interprets it brazenly as utter poker mastery. He sits at the tables that have the highest stakes and goes all in all the time, perhaps without even looking at his hand. His beginner's luck allows him to parlay a larger stack into an intensely successful (but brief) series of bluffs which catch the sharks and good players completely off guard, feeding back into the cycle and making him feel invincible. Once people figure out his game, they quickly and decisively dismantle him no matter at which table he's seated, but his brief, intensely bright, and meteoric rise is as memorable as the explosion and flameout.

It's the Company Man approach that leaves the Expert Beginner with a chance for escape. Company Man has neither Xenophobe's neurotic need to believe himself a poker expert nor Master Beginner's complete faith in his delusion, so he is the one that might actually cash out and go do something else with the money before it's all gone. There's no guarantee, but at least he has a fighting chance.

Tragicomic Explosion: Fall of the Master Beginner

The Master Beginner's fate is the least interesting because it's so entirely predictable. In the poker analogy, he blows into the high stakes table like a hurricane, creating massive disruption before blowing out just as quickly. In the real world, Master Beginners don't last, either. Their timeline is highly accelerated.

A Master Beginner that is new to a company will come in and proclaim that everything is wrong and loudly bang his own drum as some kind of messianic figure sent in to save the masses from themselves. Everyone believes him at first—even Experts. The reason is partially what I mentioned in the previous post: people assume someone this brazen must be right. But it's also partially that people in the Competent to Expert range are aware that they're not all-knowing and are inclined to accept initially at face value that someone knows things they don't.

It isn't long before the Competents, Proficients, and Experts figure out that Master Beginner is a bag of hot air. The only remaining questions then are these: (1) how long until management starts listening and acts on the words of their good developers; and (2) how many hilarious things happen before it does.

Some Master Beginners mount an impressive enough initial assault to be promoted quickly or named to a position of authority, but this just buys them a few more months or, in extreme cases, years, once the jig is up. The Master Beginner rockets through the atmosphere like a meteorite: blazingly fast, with blinding light, and ending in a spectacular conflagration.

Master Beginners are probably the least pitiable not only because they're usually insufferable personally but also because they tend to land on their feet. If one's shtick is being able to pull off a ridiculous skill bluff for a little while, securing interviews and getting job offers tends not to be a problem. Most people who know Master Beginners tend to shake their heads and say, "I can't believe people keep hiring that guy!" Master Beginner inevitably fails at his goal because his goal is to receive the recognition he deserves as a consummate Expert, and that never lasts for any length of time, wherever he goes.

Slow, Agonizing Defeat: Fall of the Xenophobe

Xenophobe's arc is a longer-playing one by far than that of Master Beginner, and there is actually some remote chance for limited success. The goal of Xenophobe is to freeze the world in its current state, within the cocoon of his comfort zone. He wants to keep the same members on the same team using the same technologies to do the same work, in perpetuity. If you're a bettor, you probably wouldn't take those odds on a long timeline. Nevertheless, that's what he aims for.

If he happens to work for some remote outfit, nestled snugly within some byzantine bureaucracy, he might be able to keep the dream alive as he runs out the clock toward retirement. But situations where nothing about the work environment changes are rare, especially in software, and they are only becoming rarer. There aren't that many opportunities to lead a team that cranks out maintenance updates to some COBOL system and plans to keep doing so until 2034.

The far more common case is that things do change. People come and go. New frameworks must be learned. New ideas sneak in through various channels, and all of it chips away at the credibility of Xenophobe's qualifications. He can manage at first, but eventually management overhears whispers from other developers who see ways of doing things that could save tons of time and money. People from other departments hear about tech buzz words and Xenophobe doesn't even know what they are. Day after day, month after month, his credibility erodes until something happens.

That something can vary. Perhaps it's the appointment of a "co-architect" or a reorganization of the group. Perhaps he's shuffled onto a different project or asked to continue to maintain the old version while an up-and-comer is tasked with architecting the rewrite. It could be outside consultants brought in as "staff augs" or farming off of whole projects elsewhere.

Interestingly, the end for Xenophobe is rarely a termination. Unlike Master Beginner, Xenophobe doesn't squirt gasoline on bridges and gleefully ignite them. He's more pitiable and shrewd. So what happens is that he's effectively put out to pasture in all but name. He might even get a better title or an office or something, but his responsibilities are divvied up and portioned out to others until he just collects a handsome wage to sit in his office and do very little.

While Xenophobe's capacity for self-delusion is high, as is generally the case with Expert Beginners, his tolerance for cognitive dissonance is extremely low. This makes this "reorg" too much for him to take lying down. He may rage-quit—a sad option since he's probably going to need to take a massive paycut to get hired anywhere else. He may simply rage, at which point his management is likely to show him a starker view of reality than he's accustomed to seeing. Or he may do neither of those things and bitterly accept the new situation.

The fate of Xenophobe is intensely depressing. If you've worked with him directly, you probably don't find it as such in the short term since he's often pretty hard to work with, but he's not a pathological grandstander like Master Beginner. He's just a guy that lucked out, believed his own hype and got out of his depth. In a way, he's like a lottery winner that squanders his fortune and winds up broke. Almost invariably, Xenophobes drift bitterly toward retirement, stripped of all real responsibility and collecting paychecks at the mercy of mid-level managers that continue to bolster (read: fake) the business case for keeping him on staff. When he's not so lucky, he winds up in the same boat as the rage-quitter—taking a huge pay and responsibility cut or crawling back to his former employer and *then* taking a huge pay and responsibility cut.

A Glimmer of Hope: The Company Man

Company Man lacks the neurotic pride of Xenophobe and the pathological cockiness of Master Beginner, and that has the potential to provide a way out. But let's consider what happens to Company Men who don't escape first. These are the ones who find their way into project management or line management and squander the false capital of their 'technical expertise.'

At the core of the Expert Beginner experience is a quest for status and recognition. It's not about money or even organizational power (beyond the software group, anyway). Truly. If it were, the Expert Beginner would never become Expert Beginner. He'd recognize that the path to a corner office usually doesn't wind its way through the land of "knowing the Java compiler inside and out." Someone interested primarily in being a C-level executive would recognize that programming is something you do for a few years and put up with until you can make the jump to project management, then line management, then VP-hood, etc. Expert Beginners relish being the best bowler in the alley and are willing to chase better bowlers away with baseball bats to protect their status if it comes down to it (or simply claim they won in spite of having a lower score, in the case of wildly delusional Master Beginner).

Company Men who don't make it fail to recognize a life raft being floated to them. Once put into a managerial position of authority, they rule like technical Expert Beginners (architects or tech leads or whatever they used to be). To put it another way, they micromanage. In their previous role, they likely had some actual programming to do or else their control wasn't absolute, so others could defy them, pick up the slack, or do what needed to be done to keep the wheels on the machine as it flew down the tracks. But a micromanaging Expert Beginner has nothing to do but meddle, bark orders, and chew people out for thinking for themselves. The wheels start to come off pretty quickly under his (mis-) management.

This Company Man unwittingly sabotages himself by finally having and exerting total technical control. Ironically, he sinks the ship by totally assuming the helm. Work stops getting done, morale plummets, projects fail, and HR issues abound as employees choose between defying the Expert Beginner and getting things right or obeying and having the project fail. Attrition mounts in these circumstances, and the Dead Sea Effect cycle time is radically accelerated with developers jumping ship like rats. Clearly, this is unsustainable, and the Company Man is demoted or let go. This is a tough spot for Company Man because he's bad at tech but has a good track record for it on paper. He could theoretically be less incompetent at managing, but he's crashed and burned in his only stab at that role. So he likely winds up hiring on as some senior developer elsewhere and trying to repeat the cycle. He isn't quite as nimble as Master Beginner, but he's not utterly trapped like Xenophobe, either. He'll move on and probably have a chance to get management right the second time around by ceasing to play at technical acumen: a face-saving strategy.

And that brings us to the successful escapee of Expert Beginnerism: the (subconsciously) self-aware Company Man. He'll never admit it, even to himself, but the successful Expert Beginner can feel the wolves closing in as the world changes and his policies are increasingly unsuccessful. As he contemplates where to go from "Architect That Frequently Squabbles with Some of his Senior Developers," this is the guy who hears a little, nagging voice in the back of his head that says, "you know, times are changing here faster than you want to, so perhaps it's time to hang up your obviously quite impressive spurs and 'retire' to management."

When he makes the jump, he also makes a clean break with his former life. He's content to be known as the guy who used to be the architect but is now in management. There will be some amount of shared, mutual fiction between him and his formerly restless techie underlings as they're grateful for his departure and earnestly wish him the best so that he stays where he's at. They'll agree with him that he was truly an awesome architect whose incredible skill set is just needed elsewhere. Everyone wins here, so why not?

And from here, there's a new period of acquisition and the slate is wiped clean. The former technical Expert Beginner reaps the benefits of being considered an 'Expert' as he embarks on a new learning curve. And while certain personality leanings make this possible, there's no guarantee that he'll become an Expert Beginner at management. He might excel in it and be receptive to continued learning in a way that he wasn't as an erstwhile techie. He might also become an Expert Beginner in management, but the odds here aren't nearly as bad since management is really a lot more subjective—competence versus incompetence is harder to assess concretely. By keeping his hands off of the ship's helm, sails, and really anything of import, the former Expert Beginner can be a decent captain by relying heavily on his competent crew, even if he was a poor sailor.

A Sad Tale

Following the career arc of Expert Beginners is really quite sad. In the early stages, one feels annoyed and a little indignant while watching advancement by luck instead of competence. As things progress, real damage is caused by poor implementation and wrong-headed approaches, resulting, for a lot of people, in stress, frustration, failure, and at times even lost jobs and failed ventures. In the end, the fate of the one that caused these things is probably poetically just, but it's hard to find happiness in. A person ill-suited for a role assumed it, caused problems, and then suffered personal hardship. It's not a great story.

CHAPTER 6

Wasted Talent:
The Tragedy of the Expert Beginner

A Sinking Ship

There are two types of sadness inherent to tragedy. Take the sinking of the *Titanic*. On one hand, the tragedy is sharply sad because hubris and carelessness led to a loss of life. But the sinking is also sad in a deeper, more dull and aching way because human nature will cause that same sort of tragedy over and over again.

The sharp sadness in the Expert Beginner saga is that careers stagnate, culminating in miserable life events like dead-end jobs or terminations. But the real, deeper sadness of the Expert Beginner's story lurks beneath the surface. The dull ache is endlessly mounting deficit between potential and reality, aggregated over organizations, communities and even nations. We live in a world of "ehhh, that's probably good enough," or, perhaps more precisely, "if it ain't broke, don't fix it."

There is no shortage of literature on the subject of "work-life balance," nor of people seeking to split the difference between the stereotypical, ruthless executive with no time for family and the "aim low," committed family type that pushes a mop instead of following his dream, making it so that his children can follow theirs.

The juxtaposition of these archetypes is the stuff that comprises awful romantic dramas starring Katherine Heigl or Jennifer Lopez. But that isn't what I'm talking about here. One can intellectually stagnate just as easily working eighty-hour weeks or intellectually flourish working twenty-five-hour ones.

I'm talking about the very fabric of Expert Beginnerism as I defined it earlier: a voluntary cessation of meaningful improvement. Call it coasting or plateauing if you like, but it's the idea that the Expert Beginner opts out of improvement and into permanent resting on one's (often questionable) laurels. And it's ubiquitous in our society, in large part because it's encouraged in subtle ways. To understand what I mean, consider institutions like fraternities and sororities, businesses that grant tenure, multi-level marketing outfits, and corporate politics with a bias toward rewarding loyalty. Besides some form of "newbie hazing," what do these institutions have in common? Well, the idea that you put in some furious and serious effort up front (pay your dues) to reap the benefits later.

This isn't such a crazy notion. In fact, it looks a lot like investment and saving the best for last. "Work hard now and relax later" sounds an awful lot like "save a dollar today and have two tomorrow," or, "eat all of your carrots and you can enjoy dessert." For fear of getting too philosophical and prying into religion, this gets to the heart of the notion of Heaven and the Protestant Work Ethic: work hard and sacrifice now to reap the benefits in the afterlife. If we aren't wired for suffering now to earn pleasure later, we certainly embrace and inculcate it as a practice, culturally. Who is more a symbol of decadence than the procrastinator—the grasshopper who enjoys the pleasures of the here and now without preparing for the coming winter? Even as I'm citing this example, you probably summon some involuntary loathing for the grasshopper for his lack of vision and sobriety about possible dangers lurking ahead.

A lot of corporate culture creates a manufactured, distorted version of this with the so-called "corporate ladder." Line employees get in at 8:30, leave at 5:00, dress in business-casual garb, and usually work pretty hard *or else*. Managers stroll in at 8:45 and sometimes cut out a little early for this reason or that. They have lunches with the corporate credit card and generally dress smartly, but if they have to rush into the office, they might be in jeans on a Thursday and that's okay. C-level executives come and go as they please, wear what they want, and have you wear what they want. They play lots of golf.

There's typically not a lot of illusion that those in the positions of power work harder than line employees: the line employees are the ones down operating drill presses, banging out code, doing data entry, crunching numbers, etc. Instead, the high-level types are generally believed to be the ones responsible for making the horrible decisions that no one else would want to make and who are never able to sleep because they are responsible for the business 24/7. In reality, they probably whack line employees without a whole lot of worry and don't really answer that call as often as you think. Life gets sweeter as you make your way up, and not just because you make more money or get to boss people around. The C-level executives put in their time working sixty-hour weeks and doing grunt work *specifically* to get the sweet life. They *earned* it through hard work and sacrifice. This is the defining narrative of corporate culture.

But there's a bit of a catch here. When we culturally like the sound of a narrative, we tend to manufacture it even when it might not be totally realistic. For example, do we promote a programmer who pours sixty hours per week into his job for five years to manager because he would be good at managing people or because we like the "work hard, get rewarded" story? Chicken or egg? Do we reward hard work now because it creates value, or do we manufacture value by rewarding it? I'd say, in a lot of cases, it's fairly ingrained in our culture to do the latter.

In this day and age, it's easy to claim that my take here is paranoid. After all, the days of fat pensions and massive union graft have fallen by the wayside, and we're in some market meritocratic renaissance, right? Well, no, I'd argue. It's just that the game has gotten more distributed and more subtle. You'll bounce around between organizations, creating the illusion of general market merit, but in reality there is a form of subconscious collusion. The main determining factor in your next role is your last role. Your next salary will probably be five to ten percent more than your last one. You're on the dues-paying train, even as you bounce around and receive nominally different corporate valuations. Barring aberration, you're working your way, year in and year out, toward an easier job with nicer perks.

But what does all of this have to do with the Expert Beginner? After all, Expert Beginners aren't CTOs or even line managers. They're, in a sense, just longer-tenured grunts that get to decide what source control or programming language to use. Well, Expert Beginners have the same approach, but they aim lower in the org chart and have a higher capacity for self-delusion. In a real sense, management and executive types are making an investment of hard work for future Easy Street, whereas Expert Beginners are making a more depressing and less grounded investment in initial learning and growth for future stagnation. They have a spasm of marginal competence early in their careers and coast on the basis of this indefinitely, with the reward of not having to think or learn and having people defer to them exclusively because of corporate politics. As far as rewards go, this is pretty Hotel California. They've put in their time, paid their dues, and now they get to reap only the meager rewards of intellectual indolence and ego-fanning.

In terms of money and notoriety, there isn't much to speak of either. The reward they receive isn't a Nobel Prize or a world championship in something. It's not even a luxury yacht or a star on the Walk of Fame. We have to keep getting more modest. It's not a six bedroom house with a pool and a Lamborghini. It's probably just a run-of-the-mill upper middle class life with one nice vacation per year and the prospect of retiring and taking that trip to Rome and Paris they've always dreamed of. They've sold their life's work, their historical legacy, and their very existence for a Cadillac, a nice set of woods and irons, a tasteful ranch-style house somewhere warm, and trans-Atlantic flight or two in retirement. And that—that willingness to have a low ceiling and that short-changing of one's own potential—is the tragedy of the Expert Beginner.

Expert Beginners are not dumb people, particularly given that they tend to be knowledge workers. They are people who started out with a good bit of potential—sometimes a lot of it. They're the bowlers who start at 100 and find themselves averaging 150 in a matter of weeks. The future looks pretty bright for them right up until they decide not to bother going any further. It's as if Michael Jordan had decided that playing some pretty good basketball in high school was better than what most people did, or if Mozart had said, "I just wrote my first symphony, which is more symphonies than most people write, so I'll call it a career." Of course, most Expert Beginners don't have such prodigious talent, but we'll never hear about the accomplishment of the rare one that does. And we'll never hear about the more modest potential accomplishments of the rest.

At the beginning of the saga of the Expert Beginner, I detailed how an Expert Beginner can sabotage a group and condemn it to a state of indefinite mediocrity. But writ large across a culture of "good enough," the Tragedy of the Expert Beginner stifles accomplishments and produces dull tedium interrupted only by midlife crises. En masse in our society, they'll instead be taking it easy and counting themselves lucky that their days of proving themselves are long past. And a shrinking tide lowers all boats.

AFTERWARD

All Is Not Lost

Dealing with Your Own Expert Beginner

I encourage you to assess what effect Expert Beginners may have on your career. You will usually see them crash and burn on a long enough timeline, if you can outlast them. Occasionally they will be promoted out of your way. Should you stick around and fight them or wait for their demise (or try to help them, if you're altruistic and masochistic)? That certainly has to be a decision for you to make, but it should help to know that even slow-acting or overly-loyal organizations will self-correct eventually, provided they have a track record for success. So consider the company, its Expert Beginner, the type of Expert Beginner, and the distance along in the process of their fall from power when you make your decision.

Avoid Becoming an Expert Beginner

If you're reading this book, it's pretty unlikely that you're an Expert Beginner. But having identified a group-(de)forming attitude that could most effectively be described as a form of hubris, I would like to propose some relatively simple steps to limit or prevent this sort of blight.

First of all, to prevent yourself from falling into the Expect Beginner trap, the most important thing to do is not to believe your own hype. Take pride in your own accomplishments as appropriate, but never consider your education complete or your opinion above questioning, regardless of your title, your years of experience, your awards and accomplishments, or anything else that isn't rational argumentation or evidence. Retaining a healthy degree of humility, constantly striving for improvement, and valuing objective metrics above subjective considerations will go a long way to preventing yourself from becoming an Expert Beginner. Also, be able to articulate your reasons for doing the things you do. Having to defend your opinions and approaches is an invaluable skill that should be kept as sharp as possible. You'll often learn just as much from justifying your approach as formulating it in the first place.

Create a Culture of Acquisition Instead of Stagnation

In terms of preventing this phenomenon from corrupting a software group, here is a list of things that can help:

1. Give team members as much creative freedom as possible to let them showcase their approaches (and remember that you learn more from failures than successes).
2. Provide incentives or rewards for learning a new language, approach, framework, pattern, style, etc.
3. Avoid ever using number of years in the field or with the company as a justification for favoring or accepting anyone's argument as superior.
4. Put policies in place that force external perspectives into the company (lunch-and-learns, monthly training, independent audits, etc.)

5. Whenever possible, resolve disputes/disagreements with objective measures rather than subjective considerations like seniority or democratic vote.

6. Create a "culture of proof"—opinions don't matter unless they're supported with independent accounts, statistics, facts, etc.

7. Do a periodic poll of employees, junior and senior, and ask them to list a few of their strengths and an equal number of things they know nothing about or would like to know more about. This is to deflate ahead of time an air of "know-it-all-ism" around anyone—especially tenured team members.

This list is more aimed at managers and leaders of teams, but it's also possible to affect these changes as a simple team member. The only difference is that you may have to solicit help from management or persuade rather than enforce. Lead by example, if possible. If it seems like a lost cause, I'd say head off for greener pastures. In general, it's important to create or to have a culture in which "I don't know" is an acceptable answer, even for the most senior, longest-tenured leader in the group, if you want to avoid Expert-Beginner-fueled group rot. After all, an earnest "I don't know" is something Expert Beginners never say, and it is the fundamental difference between a person who is acquiring skill and a person who has decided that they already know enough. If your group isn't improving, it's rotting.

Any movement toward the general betterment of society has to echo throughout the sphere of influence at which it aims; revolutions don't occur when there are only a handful of rebels. But change can come from a centrally-organized location or from the grass roots. In the case of a cultural epidemic of dues-paying and subsequent coasting, it must take the latter form since taking up the torch against complacency would be one of the most preposterous organized efforts conceivable and would likely result in draconian policies.

Expert Beginnerism as a cultural phenomenon can only be addressed by enough individuals refusing to participate. The first step is making sure that you don't become an Expert Beginner yourself. The next step is making sure your group doesn't fall victim to Expert Beginnerism. Beyond that, you simply have to talk, communicate, encourage, and lead by example. Inquisitiveness, humility, and ambition are all generally attractive qualities, and they have the capacity to be infectious. It is entirely possible to participate in turning the tide. You can prevent an Expert Beginner from infecting your groups, and you can even influence other groups, helping them not to become infected either. The battle for meritocracies and innovation is won and lost in the trenches of countless individual interactions.

About the Author

Erik Dietrich is the founder and principal of DaedTech LLC. He has a BS Degree in Computer Science from Carnegie Mellon University and a MS degree in the same from University of Illinois at Urbana-Champaign. Currently a systems architect with over ten years of experience in software architecture, design, implementation, and stabilizing/sustaining, Erik has a wide range of personal interests in addition to this area of expertise. These include home automation and home improvement, conceptual mathematics, literature, philosophy, and the sciences.